The Grail

Elizabeth Anne Hin

Cover Design and Art Copyright © 2013 by Cynthia L. Kirkwood

Editing and Book Design by Sarla V. J. Matsumura

Library of Congress Control Number: 2014933116

ISBN 13: 978-0615962405

ISBN 10: 0615962408

Printed in the United States of America

Published by Issa Press

Austin, Texas

DEDICATION

To the One, Creator of all

CONTENTS

Prologue

He walked to the Himalaya, from which he never returned, my Uncle.

I was sent to find him, which has taken these many centuries. He is the one for whom my Father lay on the cross. For no man loved another such as did he, my Father then, who would give up his life for his Brother. Let us find Yeshua's elder Twin Brother, you and I, and take my Father down from that sorrow of broken Trees.

Issa did not need to be present at the cross. Always, the first~born had been the one sought, to know God, to be beside him, to kill him, many responses to the prophecy that one was coming, that he was coming. He could know that even the Trees were not willing to be the instrument of Yeshua's death, one breath of the purpose of Issa. The Tree of Life breathed within him and within all beings, and in Issa was created the Great Mystery connected to, and connecting, all beings throughout all time and all space. We name this the Messiah, this blessing. This is present now. We are remembering his story, and Yeshua's. His breath is within all things. His Twin is taken down now, from the cross, from his sacrifice.

Part One

While all is not as it appears to be,

all is as it should be.

~Issa

I. THE WOMEN

I.1

She was not his Wife, my Mother, the Magdalene. She was wed to another, and had Children, and affluence, but was not satisfied, and challenged her era and all eras. She did not raise me, Yeshua's Child.

He was wed, too, Yeshua, to Sura, whom some call the Egyptian, she who fled to France in sorrow and exile, after her Husband's death. She raised their three beloved Children there, amid the salt marshes and birds, the desolation and sheer beauty of the Camargue, in the area named for the two women who cared for her, for beloved Sura, in their devotion to Yeshua: Des Saintes Maries, Marie Jacobe and Marie Salome.

This is our story, we women of the Christ.

J osef journeyed with his young Bride beneath the blessed Stars of Palestine, aware that her time to bear their Child was near, content to let the older Children of his early Marriage be at home with his Mother, to allow the new Marriage blossoming, reverence, and the tone of quiet conversation and rest between the older Groom and his Wife find its harmony. He was first married to the friend of his Childhood, with whom he had five Children; and when she fell ill, it was quite unreal to him, the state of a Family and home without her easy and solid temperament defining the hearth of every day. His Mother took his late Wife's place at the tasks of the woman's within their culture; and his Children grew to their own hearths, spouses and tasks, scattered through the villages within his province, with only one Son to Jerusalem, seeking a wealth and name beyond his kin.

Mary walked to the well with her Mother, Anna, and lifted a small cup to receive water for her Grandmother. This is the moment when Josef witnessed her, and knew something was one, was present, a destiny. Mary was in the beautiful time of the girl~woman, when a Child contains and expresses, embodies innocence and wisdom, and the seeking of oneness between them which might become a deep soul's signature. She found her seeking of her own life eminently safe in her Parents' home and hands. And yet, she did not expect the Angel who came to her, the one we call in history, in all three Abrahamic faiths, Gabriel.

4

When Gabriel came to Mary, he came first without words, several times. She became accustomed to the profound mood of the Divine, and then, he spoke to her in the words made famous in many translations into languages from across our human Family throughout the world: 'Hail, Mary, filled with grace, blessed art thou among women, and blessed is the fruit of thy womb.' This was a Rosary, a circlet of prayer perfect in the Divine, in all that we might name holy; and Mary was alone in a room resting when she received this naming, this blessing, this path. She was thirteen years of age.

She was with Child. In the days and months following the visitation, Mary's body transformed in grace, without her understanding. The Great Mystery of Heaven had acted through her in such a way that we have not experienced before or since, telling its own story of Heaven on Earth. She was a veritable Daughter of God, in whatever manner we might name Him, Her, That, as Yahweh, God, Allah, That Great One, Tat, the Dharmakya, Ahura Mazda, becoming Kaivalya, Ik Onkar, addressing the Kami, seeking all that we name Holy and One. And this seed, the veritable Tree of Life, which the Heavens had directly blessed into her womb as Son, began the path we have named in the Western cultures, the Messiah, sometimes the Christ.

Three months later, Mary was at the well, gathering water and conversation with the women of her village, and she experienced that something was acting within her, beyond herself. The fluttering sense she perceived within her womb had been to her a sign of life maturing as her body itself; and she felt only oneness, until this movement at the well, in which the water recognized the two souls within her womb.

There are many stories of what is true and what is not true, but there was a birth beneath a great and rare Star. Men have fought and women have sought the battles and conquests, defeats and sacrifices of their men, over jewels and lands, flags and Children, born and unborn, seeking to defend the meaning of this Star and this birth.

But this is a story of a battle that was never to be, of an era and an understanding that the Hopi name *The Great Peace;* and this story is the story beneath all Stars, including that great and rare Star, over Bethlehem, that humanity may stop fighting, and realize what we never realized, a key in the Star and the birth.

As Josef and Mary journeyed from their modest home, one Son still angry at the remarriage of his Father, Josef three decades older than the young Mary, the age really, of Josef's eldest Grandchildren. They knew the time of birth was not for two months, so that the Family home in which Mary would give birth in Egypt be safely reached. Her Child would be in no danger then of death, should the Child be a boy, as they would give birth outside of the political domain of the laws of Herod. It was her Mother's, Anna's, fervent request, knowing in her wise woman's way, that her Daughter and Grandchild were not safe entering the last months of confinement within her domain.

But the Twins came early. There was not one Babe but two. Mary's young body did not hold them within the womb until the journey safely ended at her Mother's elder Sister's home. And so, there was no room at the Inn, indeed. For the elder Twin, Issa, the one sought by humanity, was left hidden from us all, these millennia, to keep him safe from Herod; and Yeshua, the younger Son, was carried safely into the world of Osiris and Isis, and Mary's Aunt, and Uncle, and Essene prayer, and mystery.

As they passed the Southern tip of the hill toward Jerusalem, just North of the Dead Sea, Mary began to ache low in her abdomen. A sharp pain caused her to gently hold her breath, and another, and then she bled, blood upon the donkey's fur beneath her robe. She was ashamed, modest, confused, frightened, and tired, all in the most gentle and truly pure way, this young Bride, this young Daughter, this young woman of innocent, moderate, and loving ways, morals, and Family. There was no Mother here, and no midwife, no roof, no hearth, no doctor, no wise woman nor man. Josef and his young Wife were in the midst of a journey that was to carry humanity in this land of the River Jordan, between homes for two millennia, until her Sons were delivered safely, truly, to her, to their Father, and to humankind.

For Josef, his five Children had all been born as naturally as the Sun rising, with the cries of labor tended by Family women and village women, until he came to his first Wife, fatigued yet flushed with the color of joy and new life upon her face, within her eyes, and in the Babe presented to him, cleansed and comforted from within her arms, from her bosom. This was a woman's World. And here, at the North of the Negev, a young woman of infinite trust in her own Father and Mother, in her Husband, in her life, and in life itself, faced the spots of blood upon the donkey's back, which she could not brush away, and knew she must find a woman who could care for this bleeding. She knew the birth coming was stronger than her understanding.

And so, climbing that hill Westward toward the valley South of Jerusalem, they asked the Bedouin, 'Is there a wise woman for a young Mother, for whom the Babe will not come for two months?' And any woman of age seeing this realized, a wise woman is needed, so that there is not death or trauma of the Mother or the coming Babe.

Finally, a shepherd, a man of Josef's age, confided to him that with this blood, with a Mother very young, with a lack of wisdom about birth in such a young woman, there was sometimes death. He knew that the wisest woman for birth all about the hills was an Innkeeper's Wife, in Bethlehem, to the South, at the outskirts of Jerusalem. That they must go. And so they did.

Such Saints are not part of the stories we often have told of our histories, as humans, as warriors, as seekers of culture, as seekers of faith; but these Saints mark our every day upon this Earth, and always have. Their signatures show our souls and lives the path of the Stars.

It took them almost three long, long days, for Josef understood the wisdom of the elder shepherd. They traveled eighteen hours each of these days, until Mary's body began an ache that heralded the Star about to be born from her womb.

At the Inn, the wise woman turned and knew that something was coming, someone was coming. Her Husband was accustomed to this, to her warm, wise care tending fevers, Brides, tempers, losses, deaths of illness and infirm old age, and

10

birth, her body the very baulm of the breath of life itself. She was as content to regard a sparrow's nest and the first standing step of a young calf, colt, or puppy, kitten or lamb, as to hold a hand through the last breath of an elder sage villager of small farm and spinning wheel. She knew the breath of life; she knew holy breath was calling to her. She turned and set down the cloth in her arms. Blessedly for us all, her Husband and her region trusted her nature and held her in her wisdom and humble life. She walked through the threshold, saw the couple from a distance, and waited. She knew that life and death were approaching her, and she tended life. She was a woman of comprehensive strength and of all faith, of human endeavor and experience. She saved, for us all, the Twins, and their Mother. How may we ever thank her?

A nd so the birth came. Twins, both boys. Issa, Yeshua. But we do not know Issa's story. We do not tell this. His mystery is the Great Mystery, for he is the one we have sought, not for himself but for the key of Heaven on Earth which turns through his soul and heart, through his heartbeat.

He was born first. And then, Yeshua. No one had known that there were two, come early with the weight and pressure on their fourteen year~old girl~woman Mother, too much blood lost on the journey from the Jordan Valley to Bethlehem. So, the first~born was kept from her breast. He was larger, slightly stronger, and the wise woman knew that the young Mother was injured by the birth, as well as fulfilled, delivered of her Sons, these Sons. Nursing one would call her body to resolve; nursing two might call to too little strength in the months and years to come. So, the wise woman took the first~born, and chose for him, fed him milk from her cow, goat, sheep; and he was calm beneath the Star. They all slept.

Josef and Mary, and the second~born, nestled and rested through the first dawn and the second and another, the wise woman sending Josef to her Husband, to give the woman private time to bathe the young Mother, to poultice the opening to Mary's womb, to salve ointment onto her breast, to hold fortifying drink to her lips. She kept the second~born at Mary's side, to call the young Mother to rest and heal, to tend and nurture.

After the fourth day, she believed the Mother would live, beyond the weakness of lost blood before the birth, beyond infection, beyond homesickness for Mary's own Mother, home, hearth, and kin; resting, as it were, in a peasant's home, in the manger beneath the home proper, where the animals and foods were stored, lying upon rough cloth, straw and wood, not the spun toiles of her Mother Anna's work, not her mattress, not her bed, no dish nor vase, no pictures nor windows, no prettiness here, but earth and animals, hills and Stars. And a wise woman and her strong devout Husband. And Josef.

And so the men came, and tricked my Grandmother. Two were wise, and one of the two, apprenticed a tender helper, a young man as spiritual Son, to learn wisdom and to inspire all throughout history with his pure heart, his effervescent spirit seeking God in Starlight and wildflower, in the humor of camels spitting and women flirting at oases and village squares. For he was handsome, the apprentice, and they were mysterious, these two men of the sacred, journeying to follow a Star to find someone, something of which they would not speak.

The third was famed in this land and throughout, as were the other two, and one night after all were asleep, he attempted to seduce the apprentice, who awoke with a cry, a cry that should have warned the other two wise men, but did not suffice. The third quietly removed himself and returned to his own bedding, and this was not spoken of again until now.

The apprentice was not as a toy, an instrument for sexual play and humor and charm, but a spiritual Son to his mentor. Whether men and women believe that men can be together with men, and women with women, in the temperaments sometimes created by Heaven, just as Heaven ordains amber eyes or locks of hair curled, waved or straight, or height, or length of one's years; the unwilling seduction of a youth, whether young man or young woman, is not at peace in any soul.

And they, the three men and spiritual Son, found the Husband of the wise woman. He noted that his Wife was present, with one of the Babes. She was with Issa, carrying him about. At first, the three journeying men thought the Babe noted was the Husband's, that two Children had been born to two women, a Babe to the wise woman, and a Babe to Mary. They turned to Josef and Mary, Yeshua at her breast, and began to attend the one whom they thought they had sought beneath the Star. But Josef noted that he had two Sons, two new Sons, together with his grown youths thriving, blooming, the Sons and Daughters of his late Wife. And the third man walked to the wise woman and noted that he wished the wisdom of the Child carried by her, he wished the destiny, the mantle, the knowledge of Heaven, to be the Tree of Life in this elder Son, the one whom they truly sought. And the wise woman knew this man was wounded in his soul and life.

So, we talk about the gifts the wise men journeying from the East brought to Yeshua: gold, frankincense and myrrh, prayer, ceremony, and recognition. And, we do not speak of the first students of Issa, the wise men and the wounded, for Issa to see home to their paths in Heaven on Earth. For the gifts of the wise men were given to Yeshua, and he was held, and perfumed, with incense burned about him, wrapped in new cloth as is the tradition, and celebrated in food and drink taken after, in the way of humanity partaking of a repast to mark, to note, a ceremony of life or death. Yeshua was blessed. And Issa remained in the care of the wise woman, swaddled at her side. And the third man noted that he wanted what this Child was, he wanted to know Heaven.

And the wise woman quietly withdrew to the rooms above, where she dwelled with her Family, and turned her entire being, all of her strength, all of her soul, to prayer, in the manner of the prayer of her Father's Family, the Prayer of Osiris. She offered the Baby, Issa, the first~born, to this.

And she sent her Son for Mary's Mother, Anna.

Anna and Mary Salome placed their homes in the care of their loved ones, embraced their Husbands, and turned through the threshold to Bethlehem. A journey of this way might take six weeks, seven, should the Babe have been stillborn, should the Mother have died, be dying, should the Babe be handicapped, should Josef not wish to take the Babe, so many ways might there be for the elder women to bear. Two weeks, seven, six, four...

Coins tied into their skirts, two changes of clothing, camel bags, ointment, unguent, a new shawl for Anna's Daughter, woven by her Mother through the months of the coming Babe, needles and handkerchiefs, the timeless joys of human life worn within the days of women everywhere. They set forth in fear, for there was no word but that the Child had tried to come early, and that the Grandmother, the Mother of the young Mother, was called.

Anna was called to Mary. All along the Jordan Valley, that beautiful valley which should be only of abiding peace and harmony among all peoples, these two kind and strong women journeyed in fear.

They crossed the hill to the peasant home, and Anna's heart found great loss when she saw the lower door open, a sparrow at its entry, hay through the threshold at the floor. She realized her Daughter lay here, without window, without linen embroidered at the window, without clean cloth, without wildflowers in a Phoenician vase of tinted glass, and without her. She prepared herself to meet a corpse, of Daughter, of Grandchild. Her heart turned hard toward Josef, whom she should not have allowed to take her Daughter this way, but have left Mary to bear the Child with the women of their Families.

With slender hand at the doorwell, Mary stepped into the sunlight, and Anna could hardly bear her heart. It must be the Child, stillborn, or not lived soon after the birth, born unwell, or with anomaly. Mary Salome called to Mary, arm raised in greeting, and Mary turned to see her Mother, and rested in the women of her clan.

As Anna held the Babe, Yeshua, the wise woman came into the stable, and gesturing, beckoned for Anna to come, alone, with her. They entered the rooms of the wise woman, and the wise woman turned, lifted a Babe, wrapped in swaddling clothes, and laid him in his Grandmother's arms. And through the wise woman, Anna knew, 'This is the first~born, the one whom Herod would kill.' And the wise woman left the room.

'Oh, Issa,' Anna named him in that moment.

She did not carry him to her Daughter but stayed with the Babe, and then brought Mary Salome to him. She stated that Salome would journey with Mary, who needed her. And then Anna prepared to return home, to raise her Grandson, Issa, no one ever knowing on the records of taxes, in the annals of time, that this Son of the Star had been born to humanity.

II. THE UNKNOWN

II.1

I ssa turned, saw his Grandmother, who was his Mother in life, and knew that he was safe, well, true, and good. He was four, and, awakening from his nap, expressed the Logos as himself, ever aware of his Twin and himself as a constellation of the Lord in all of the Lord's names, across the Universe of men and deer, of bloom and crescent Moon. She taught him and told him, this word of our language, this moral, this shirt, sit up here, this gesture with food, with Elder, with penis to urinate, with oil or water and cloth to clean, and now to bed.

There was no man. His Grandfather had left the beautiful story, the rare story, of his time away to pray, when there were no Children so many years. The Grandfather, Anna's late Husband, had come home once, to find his Wife, mature now, married to him for some years, tired from the women's unkindness that they had no Child, that there must be something wrong, with her, with him, with them, that God in all his names must not be with them; they must not be blessed. How sad. He grew angry at her pain, his darling, and spoke to some of the men of this,

21

over glasses of tea, in the gathering men will do, to converse in their ways; and he found that the men too, were somewhat troubled that the Lord had given them no progeny, that they must not be blessed.

And he went to a tender place~ you could find it now, should you journey Jerusalem way, just as you could find Eliah's cave, and where one Prophet walked, and another, all in their footsteps of prayer and life, of dates and figs wrapped in cloth, of nut, fruit and honey, naps beneath occasional Trees, of limestone, of wellspring, and always in the humble practice of regarding the will of That Great One in all names.

His Grandfather visited this place for three days, and three days became a sacred image for Issa, for his Grandmother taught him to revere God, that God had answered his Grandfather's prayer, and had brought to Anna a Child when the Grandfather returned from his journey, a Babe, his Mother, Mary, to an old man, and to an old woman, to them, his Grandparents, whom God had blessed.

His Grandmother taught him in this way, through story, which the Christians name parable, for there was no man to show him to live a holy story, to be the living faith, the courage to live a sacred way; so she showed him through the stories of her late Husband, whom she loved.

And Issa understood, and he became the Word incarnate.

His days were full of birdsong and moral, of trust and task. He carried what his Grandmother could not, and respected her manner of day and night, of Spring and heat, and cool toward Winter, adage of scorpion and dove, or this food and that color, this bargain for fabric and thread, that conversation of kindness and goodness toward all peoples, for all peoples held a spark of God, would not his Grandfather have known that within all men, if he were still here beside them? And Issa knew this was true. He had a real Angel, the soul of his Grandfather, in Song, story and virtue, taught him in adage and gesture, every day, by Anna.

So Issa grew, unafraid, knowing Heaven in all things, in all moments, in all beings. He was content and good. And the men knew him to be the blessed Son of Mary. For he was the blessed Grandson of his Grandfather and of Anna. He was Silent when he was learning, and let the contentment, the peace of God, teach him in all ways. This Word was everywhere, eternal, from God in all of His names, in all souls, in all of creation, and the key turned, this soul, this boy, this man.

This key, Issa.

He was raised without his Mother's touch, without Mary's milk, the milk of her breast and the touch of her hair, skin, her scent, from her tender, strong and supple body which bore him.

He was raised with her Mother's touch, Anna's touch, and the milk of cow and sheep, and the touch of the wind, the light of the Sun, the blue of the sky, and the water of the well. And the Word that he is grew strong and true, clear and unafraid, with a shy introspection known only to his soul and the Creator Who caused Issa to be. For Anna knew to raise him with teaching, ethic and story, tradition and virtue, habit and moral, manner and prayer. And she knew that he was born of mystery, mystery beyond her Daughter, her own late Husband, and herself. And to that mystery she was true.

For prayer, they tended the Synagogue of her village; for work, she allowed him the privilege of observation and practice beside the elder men who were the colleagues of her late Husband. And Issa learned what it is to be a good man from a minion of men surrounding his home, up a small hill, along a quiet path, down into a near valley, men who were wise, or simple, or strict or not so. A complexity arose within him, woven of their ways, their wisdom and their dignity, as souls, as men, as human beings.

24

And when he was of age, she took him to the Temple Mount, where the elder Rabbi, seeing this boy~man without Father or Mother, but brought by his maternal Grandmother, assumed an orphan, and blessed Issa into manhood, asking Heaven's protection, silently expressing grief, and hope, that the promise of this young man's soul might be fulfilled, realized, ordained before the gates. And he anointed Issa.

Issa's favorite of all the men was still, like himself, with the sweet turn of mouth, twinkle and slightly upward wrinkle at the corner of eye, marked by a life of kindness and light humor, metaphor and tolerance, gratitude and forbearance, in mercy and in healing.

The Healer taught Issa of the Seasons of the year, of the Seasons of a domestic animal's life, of the planting of crops, their tending and harvesting, of herbs, of traded ointments, of the Seasons of grace, birth, lust, love, pregnancy, birth, life, age, and death, in the scarab and the snake, the ram and the wren, the horse and the cat, and in the human being.

With each lesson, each day on which he addressed Issa, the Healer imparted a question, 'How shall we be with this, my Son?'

And the Healer remained silent. And Issa answered him in the Silence. And the Word was made flesh.

Issa embodied the answers, which arose within his soul and sang through his body made of starlight and sunbeam, spring water and wheat. The Healer shepherded the Word, and never told him of the death of his own Son, the death from which no one thought the Healer would recover, until Anna had brought Issa to the well, when a newborn, and having opened the infant Issa onto a blanket while she gathered water and spoke with the women, she had quietly acknowledged, 'And how shall I, an elder widow, raise a Son?'

Speaking thus, she had regarded the Healer, whose eyes of vast grief, in response, regarded Anna. And Issa was raised by the two of them, in their two lives, and by a village, and a blessed land.

Issa realized Silence as his greatest prayer. In Silence, he knew, in the stillness of the Universe, that the Creator would answer Himself, as He did in river and mountain, Sun and cloud, candle flame and moonlight, breeze and storm. Issa found the greatest peace in nature, in innocence, in the Seasons, in the Elders' care, in the seeking of relationship with Him in the work of one's cycle of life: digging a well, watching wool sheared, spun, woven, sewn, buying a basket for Anna from an elder woman at a village too far for his aged Grandmother to walk, watching her thresh, carrying a scythe, smelling the coming rain, running the harvest of grain through his holy palms.

He found that contentment and true meaning were his signature. Although he was specific in his gestures, he was without judgment; he held all of life as sacred, and sought the signature of his Creator in every breath and moment, his life a Song of God in all of His names, of all that has ever been, is and ever shall be. He knew this was the true path of a man, any man, and he walked the path.

Issa listened. And the Silence was everywhere. And always answered him.

II.5

A nd then one day Issa knew a stillness in the Silence, and he was discontent. He arose to find that there was no water from the well; Anna was still abed. And he quietly walked to the well, alone, gathered water, composed their small cooking fire, and tenderly arranged the cover over his beloved Grandmother's shoulders and body.

Later, as Sun turned toward dusk, he walked to the Healer's home, and sat, still, discontent for the first time in his young man's life.

He was Silent in all of this.

His protector was dying.

The Sun rose and set upon the hearth of Anna for almost two cycles of the Moon, and as the Moon drew full for the second time, her breath entered the Silence that is ever Issa's home in God. And Issa was beside her body, her soul, and her life, in Silence to the well each day, changing the cloths of her body and her bed, cooking the foods she had fed him, nourishing her as she had him, in all ways, each day of their life thus far.

He expressed to his Grandmother that the protection of her for his soul and life would continue in every breath of his own body, fulfilled in him as her Grandchild. The fire lit, the window closed at night against damp chill, the door opened at dawn for the sweet soothing sound of the dove, the hart hunted by two of the village men and traded, so that a roast and stew might warm her body and strengthen them both as she moved into death.

And in the middle of a night, between the dark and the dawn, as Issa sat beside her, true and free, her last breath entered the blessing of Issa's Silence in God, and he saw His beloved Anna home into her Creator.

II.7

And Issa never left the Silence.

A nd Issa never left the path his Grandmother, Anna, wove as a sacred weaving through all the moments of their days and nights together. He dwelled as her Grandson and his path was perfect in God.

And Josef sent for him, his Son, first~born of the Twins. Herod was no longer alive and there was no reason for the Twins to be separate. Josef wished to know this Son, Issa, and wished to please God by caring for him.

I ssa did not go until he had grieved.

And, until he had honored.

In the Silence that is his home, he tended daily life for a full cycle of twelve Moons, as is the Jewish custom, and he dwelled in reverence, respecting all daily and nightly actions which his Grandmother and her chosen mentors had taught to him. He continued to learn at the feet and at the side of the men to whom she had entrusted him, shearing wool, hammering wood, repairing three leaks in a mentor's roof, placing stone and board where animals had broken through a fence, drying grain, trading for new cloth, tending a Wedding.

He kept the lace cloth atop Anna's small table, and her favorite stoneware pitcher with cool well water. He swept, and cleaned, fished, and shepherded, and listened, to Heaven, in all ways.

After the year's cycle, he moved to his Grandmother's bed, and let her clothing be given to the women of his mentors' Families, and he prepared to answer his Father's request to him.

I ssa tended two matters composed of his own Silence in God.

He journeyed to the Temple Mount of Jerusalem, and ordained a ceremony for his Grandmother, Anna, with the elder Rabbi, the Priest who had blessed him into his manhood. Issa brought money which he had saved, and items of offering, sacred to the altars of the Priests, to honor Anna in all the gates, of all the Temple, and of all Jerusalem, and of all the land, and of all the World.

From Jerusalem, Issa returned to Anna's and his home.

At the breaking of dawn, he walked in Silence to the Healer's home, and from the Silence in which Issa dwells, Issa told the Healer, 'You are my spiritual Father.' And he placed a handsome shawl of finest wool he had purchased in Jerusalem at his spiritual Father's lap.

Issa had birthed Children, buried Elders, tended the diseased and the infirm; and he had nursed wounds and animal bites, infestations, emotional conflicts and confusions; and all of these wisdoms were learned in tenderness and faith, always in the Silence of God, at the side of his spiritual Father, the Healer.

In the Silence of God, he embodied his Grandmother and his spiritual Father.

His walk took three days, to the home of Josef and Mary, and his younger Twin, Yeshua, and their younger siblings. Issa observed a falcon, hunting high over the desert, the leaves of Trees turned slightly downward, cupped inward, as rain had not fallen for several months in this driest of Seasons in the cycle of the year. He broke bread at twilight in gratitude and grace, as he made camp, supped Olive and Date, spring water from his goat stomach flask, and rested. Beneath the Star of Bethlehem he rested, this elder Twin, Twins of the Star of Bethlehem incarnate.

The turning toward heat and light of the dawn hour, Songbird at near Tree, morning Star still a~sky, called him awake toward the home of his Father and Mother.

In Silence.

II.13

Yeshua turned and there was Silence. He knew this Silence; he remembered. And then, over the rise, he remembered.

He remembered as a tall figure rose over the rise, still in his mood, steady in his footstep, unafraid, serene, internally poised.

Yeshua went to fetch his Mother.

The mood was that of late Autumn, before the rains, as the Family partook a Sabbath meal together. Mary covered her hair with a soft cloth, and turning toward the East, to the direction from which the Sabbath Sun would dawn, she lit an Olive oil lamp at table, and blessed the bread, and called her Family to their blessed meal, and their blessed company.

Josef sat, sad, and fulfilled, his third Son now at table with his fourth Son and with his younger Children. As he had let the Children of his first Marriage find their homes and pathways, so he had let Issa, from birth.

Mary turned to her Husband's wisdom and allowed the men their ways, their habits, their work, their rest and leisure. Issa was formed. He could caretake aspects of the work for which Josef was too old, now, but so could and might and did Yeshua. There was no need for two Carpenters.

And the world had need of a Healer.

After two nights of rest, nights both calm and fretful, to Issa's Silence an elder woman came; she came to Josef and Mary's door. Would the young Son come, the young man, some kin to Josef and Mary, and Yeshua, anyone could see it, he and Yeshua were almost like Twins, would he come? For we have heard that he is trained by the Healer. Could he come? Could he come now? Right away.

Neither Josef nor Mary answered before, out of the Silence, Issa arose, and nodding to the woman and to Josef and to Mary, he gathered a small bag and a light cloak.

And the man whom he healed was suffering. Unto death. The man had crossed the River Jordan into that beautiful land, trading silver and metal wrought into jewelry and implements, and, stopping on the way back, deeply thirsty, had drunk from a shallow ditch of water fouled by animals. And in strong fever, his entire body was tormented. This had transpired for many days, and his elder Mother knew that without intercession, her beloved Son would not live.

Entering the home, Issa came to the young man's side, and from the Silence within himself and all around him, he took the young man's burning hand, smelled his body, perceived his skin and eyes, lips, and tongue, and heard his anguished breathing. In all of his senses, he, who never left the mystery of Father, Mother, Creator in Heaven from whom he was birthed, That Great One whose name is too holy to speak, and who has been named many names by all peoples of the world, sought grace. And he, who was raised by his Mother's Mother, Anna, and he, who was shepherded by the Healer, knew, in the Great Mystery of which we all are one, all are Children, all are vulnerable and pure, and turned to the Mother, and spoke, 'I will return.'

II.17

In the dark of that night, Issa returned, and, mixing a tea, placed with infinite tenderness yet firm strength, that tea into the mouth of the young man. Issa held him into the crook of his shoulder against himself, much as he would a small yearling lamb to be shorn for the first time. Much the way he might gentle a young woman giving birth. He bathed the man's face, and feet, and hands, his genitals, and anus and belly, his back and shoulders and chest. He lifted the young man while the Mother placed clean hay or straw and cloth beneath her Son, and he covered the young man with a clean cloth.

And the man was healed.

II.18

Was it the Hyssop or the late Autumn berry known only to the Bedouin, or the rare grass seed, or the honey? Was it the breezes of and baulm of night air blessing the young man's breath, as Issa prayed all across his desert quest those several hours, seeking blessing for this young man, this young man's elder Mother's only Son, to be spared, to dwell in longevity and grace and goodness? Was it the Healer's recipe and wisdom blessed as mantle to Issa as spiritual Son and heir?

Out of the Silence he was healed, this young man, Tomas, out of the Silence.

Conversations began at the well, in the village, at the loom, at the Grape press, at the Carpenter's bench. A Child was born safely and to a slender~hipped girl of thirteen, breech, after eight days and nights of crying and labor. An old man slipped quietly away in natural breath, natural death, his pain from cancer so intense for so many months that no one thought a kind death possible for his tragic body. He slipped away with hand held in his Wife's. A last quiet breath, his eyes regarding her, filled with love. And a broken leg of a young boy, bound, healed. From a bone intensely piercing the skin, the leg devastated beneath him, the boy's bone was bound, the skin poulticed and baulmed. The boy could walk again, play again, somewhat compromised, but alive, and with two strong legs.

It is Yeshua. No, it is someone else, so like him. No, it is Yeshua. No.

Yeshua asked of Josef whether he might study the works of sacred men. And Josef knew the day had come when the tools of a Carpenter were not a language strong enough for these Sons born beneath the Star of Bethlehem, this second Twin who was anointed by men from the East. And Josef responded to Yeshua that when it was Josef's time, his Father's time, Yeshua might journey to the Persian, the one who had anointed him, and to his Priests of Zoroaster, but not alone.

Late Spring, as blossom turned to Apricot and Peach and Plum, the mood of most turned to Summer love and open windows and doorways, clothing and hair freshly washed, and babes of Springtime from lamb to puppy, chick to burro, growing in harmony and play, the plantings having taken in fields, the young Olives and Grapes appearing in bounty on the branch and vine.

Issa paused one evening, and in his breath, in the tawny amber of his tender eyes, in the sentience and kindness wrought by Heaven in every cell, from sinew to vein, he knew that his Father had stopped breathing. And the tenderness in him became paramount, quietly attending Mary's needs, and Yeshua's.

And Josef's.

II.22

From that breath forward, Issa shepherded. His Father, Josef, his Mother, Mary, his Twin, all. In Silence did the man arise, to take his place upon this Earth, as his Father, Josef, prepared to leave Earth for Heaven, the Heaven which is Issa's home.

Issa arose in the morn, fresh with the dew, and tended that day, and the eve, and the rest, the rest of the night. And then the next. He was in the Silence he had always known, and yet he was a man, now.

On the day that Josef first drew the palm of his hand, for a moment only, to the left side of his chest, Issa noted. He strode to his Father's side and took in his arms the wood with which his Father was working.

As Josef's gesture of palm to chest became common, and the strain at Josef's eyes, and the slight tenor of strain in his breath, and the tension in his left arm and in his shoulders, and his lack of thirst, and his slower rising in the morn, Issa cared for the chores. Until one night he went to Mary, who was outside in the late Summer evening visiting with several of the women. In Silence, and, taking her hand, he led his Mother home to Josef and, placing her hand in Josef's, Issa went to his bed.

These were tender days, tender weeks, in which the villagers saw Josef walk with his Mary upon the crest, and linger late into the evenings, beneath the Stars, in the soft, blessed Autumn light turning toward night. They walked, and talked, and he brought for her a soft mauve rose shawl of finest wool, which Issa sent for from a merchant he knew of, in Jerusalem.

One might have believed them a young couple in the full bloom of courtship, did one not know the decades of holy life this precious couple had thus lived.

And Issa woke Yeshua early in the morns and the Twins worked together, side by side, as they had been conceived, and born; and allowed their Parents respite, this sacred time, together.

For three days Issa remained quiet in his breath, attentive to the Silence everywhere, everywhere. Each day, as evening deepened into night, and all of the Family, animals, flowers and birdsong turned toward rest, he arose, and at the hearthroom, his own breath became an almost silent strength to his Father's breath as the Patriarch prepared to leave his body.

The third night, just at the darkest hour, as Issa sat at the hearth, he built a fire, and awakened his Mother, and placed her shawl over her shoulders, and placed her hand in his Father's; and they sat beside Josef.

And as the dawn sky turned blooming into the day, Josef's soul turned to Heaven, and Issa's breath and soul rested in the Silence that was his home, and Mary wept, at peace, in the infinite mercy of her Husband's last days.

And after the burial of their sacred Father, good and true man, to all, and offerings made to the Temple in his name, and remembrances, Issa and Yeshua turned to the care of their Mother. And the Silence in Issa was aware of the turning of Yeshua toward a sacred path, a path of the soul and not of the Carpenter's tools.

II.26

Issa came into the home one morning, late, for the midday meal, only to find his Mother, Mary, crying. No, weeping. He had missed the moment when his Twin asked their Mother that Yeshua might journey to the East to seek wisdom and ways of the sacred men from his birth.

And the breath in Issa knew that his Twin was in danger, for he had not experienced the oneness of the conversation of his Twin with his Mother until he saw Mary's tears.

And he stated to Mary, from the Silence in which he dwells, 'I will go with him, Mother.'

As Yeshua prepared for the journey, the journey which his Father promised to him, Issa expressed gratitude in prayer and practice, for the Healer, his Spiritual Father, and for Josef, his Father.

Issa turned his grateful Silence to the Winter ways of wool to the loom for the women to card and spin and weave, and the trade of carpentered items and work for feed full of protein for the animals at full coat, and water in the cistern, and fish to the drying racks, and meat to the butcher and to salt, and flour from the miller.

He prepared all that must be tended for the time they would be gone, these Twins; and he arranged that the elder of their Sisters and her Husband would care for Mary these many months to be.

II.28

everal days before their planned departure, Issa came quietly to Mary, and tenderly gestured for his Mother to sit at her bed. They were alone in the home.

He placed at her hands new cloth, and sacred items, and a baulm for her hands, a perfumed oil, and a bag of coins, half of all given to him over many years from his healing work, and a beautiful shell of the Sea, which he loved above all things.

He placed the shell in her holy hands, with infinite tenderness, and to his blessed Mother, from the Silence in which he dwells, Issa said, 'I will bring him home to you, Mother.'

Part Two

Split a piece of wood, I am there.   Lift up the stone and you will find me there.

~The Gospel According to Thomas

III. THE JOURNEY

III.1

Two bags were packed by Issa, two bags. For he knew that something was wrong, amiss, and he packed the bag of a Healer first. And then, his own.

The first he packed in the very manner taught him by the Healer. He knew the blessing of his spiritual Father, and Josef, and all Fathers, and the One who made them, would preserve him and bring him the wisdom he needed and sought, for the path before him, and his younger Twin.

III.2

They departed before the light of the East rose, before the Sun; and their Mother turned to the home of her Daughter to take rest and refuge for the many months to come, a sojourn of quest and grace

.

III.3

Yeshua turned to the dawn, to the Stars, to the moonrise, to the mountains, to the desert, to the sands, to the oases, to the birds. He was a Child of the world, a young man of innocence, pure and good.

At the night fire, he spoke with Issa about the day, the land, the quest, the questions, the wisdom of Great Mystery he knew, and the language and depth with which he sought to apply this most precious gift, the gift of being a Son of Heaven.

III.4

And Issa was steadfast beside his younger Twin, in the Silence of Heaven in which he dwelled.

They partook of honey, so fine, and bread of a semolina unknown to their villages, small river fish, sundried and salted, black figs, small fine dates and a small citrus fruit, stews of lamb and broth, rich and fragrant with herbs known and unknown to the two, and deep well and spring waters.

They were comforted by new blankets woven of stripes of camel hair, so warm, so strong, soft yet fulfilling, as the nights turned deeper in length and frost came with the break of day.

Buildings turned to arched entryways, labyrinthine adobe and screened windows of woven woods, and women to a greater shyness, a privacy, veiled from the men of the outside, and Children, kept within a more private way.

Everywhere the Twins went, women, Children and Elders observed them shyly, and men welcomed them nobly and privately in the dignity of their own ways and the dignity of the Twins' countenance and manner.

With one clear tender nod of a village leader, they were welcomed to sit with the men beneath a grove of five great Cedar Trees as they passed through his village. Another day, in another place, they were called to a meal with several branches of a Family, and shared prayer and food. They smoked tobacco from a great handwrought water pipe and slept that night with the fragrance deep in their hair and beards and hearts.

They purchased fragrant attar of Agarwood for their toilette, and tasted water flavored with the oil of Orange Blossoms, and they were well, and their journey was blessed and beautiful.

III.6

The first wise man they sought was Syrian, so revered, so merciful, that their time with him was a blessing beyond all words. He was in his last years, and they all knew that grace alone had allowed them the blessing of this second meeting, the first having been an anointing at the birth of the Twins.

He imparted to them two virtues: a prayer, a prayer which included all, all peoples, all of creation, everywhere, and all time, all Seasons, all that has ever been, and all that is and all that shall ever be. And his articles for anointing, which he placed into the hands of Issa.

Out of the first, Yeshua awoke with the dawn and spoke, 'Abba, thou art in Heaven, thy name is hallowed before all men…' and 'You, who have ever been, and who will ever be….' And Yeshua was deep and content, and filled with holy meaning, for the quest which he sought was answering him in prayer and life, this sacred path which he had always known as his to seek, to be, to live, to become.

Out of the second, Issa placed the cherished articles for anointing within his bag of a Healer together with a gently cloth~wrapped bracelet of Syrian silver for his Mother, Mary.

As they crossed the vast deserts and lands of stardust and saffron, silk and tent, rug and caravan, story and tea, freedom and firelight, wellspring and tribe, they were aware that they were holy and humble, and safe in the grace of the One who had sent them, the One who had sent all men, and all creatures and all mountains and seas, all storms and winds, and calm nights, and Spring rains, and soft flowers.

They came to know that all men sought the same truth, and the same One, whom the Twins' language had forever named Abba, who was named many names throughout the Earth, and that beyond all ways there was a way, and that way was to be embodied by the Twins in all ways for all days.

III.9

That way was kind to Children of all lands, and infinite in caretaking the infant and the deeply pregnant, and tender with the dying and the deeply aged, and gracious and sweet to the women and girls of every age at every well and at turns in the road and traders' places of rest, meeting them with baskets of figs and dried meats and fruits, and skins filled with water flavored with mint and herb to keep it safe and clean.

That way was story at night in village and town, oasis and campsite, wherein one Elder would tell a story, of history from his people, for the sake of teaching all in the camp's circumference, a needed virtue, and counseling wisdom that one not fall from grace. A translator would be present from the village or nearby, or a fellow traveler who knew several languages, or aspects of them, to speak well, eloquently, or with difficulty, the stories from near and afar so that all might understand, and share, and be together as one, in the many, in the One.

That way was also the way of virtue, the path taught by Anna, and Mary, and Josef, and the Healer, that which one is to do and be and become, a good man, a true man, a virtuous woman, a noble woman, of soul, and heart, and life, in all ways, all his days, all her days.

III.11

There was a storm, of wind and sand for three days. The sky turned so deeply, life was at rest in the ways of the One and of time immemorial upon this Earth, wherein the men from the oasis taught Issa and Yeshua how to cover their heads and bodies, to stay with their bodies low, with their backs to the wind, in the tent, and with their breath very quiet as if sleeping to stay alive through the storm. And they did.

III.12

nd then another storm came, unsought.

I n Persia, they came into the city on a clear fine day, the storm having refreshed the climate for hundreds of miles all around, peoples of every tribe so content to have the fineness of Spring and the safety of life restored. The second of the men, the wise men who journeyed to the Star of birth, was no longer upon our Earth. And so, the Twins sought the place of the third wise man who had come to them at their time of birth. They sought to pay honor, and for Yeshua to seek the teachings of the sacred for which he knew he had been born.

Issa was led to a room by the Wife of the wise man, and Yeshua to another, and they bathed and rested and came to the evening meal. The man took a great interest in Yeshua, which caused Issa dis~ease, yet he knew only that this man wanted a boy for his lover, even though this man had a Wife and Children, and here in this very house.

He was certain that Josef had taught Yeshua to take care of himself in these matters and to turn away, and he went to rest that night certain in the safety of their lives in the One, blessed beneath the Stars of the very places in our World where mathematics, astronomy, and so many arts and sciences were forged in prayer and practice, in thought and heart, and in life itself.

III.15

In the very dark of the night, from within his sleep, Issa realized he was not in the Silence, but drugged, and he strove to be One in the Silence that is his home.

III.16

Out of the drugs he came awake into the dawn, and rose to his Brother's side and found him with blood on his bedding and fear in his eyes, and a break in his soul and heart. He bathed his Brother, and dressed him, and they left from this unholy place, in Silence, without a word, these Sons who are the Word of the One, wounded, and true.

And Issa journeyed almost two hours strongly beside Yeshua, in Silence, beside the breezes and the late Spring blooms, lambs and puppies, open windows, and women sorting, weaving and embroidering cloth.

The Twins did not stop until Issa found a place in which the Silence in him was able to be fully present, and could know himself beyond enraged, beyond quavering, beyond loss, beyond judgment, beyond regret, beyond argument.

At this place he entered the Silence exhaling and inhaling; knew grace, gathered his Healer's bag to his side and brought forward an unguent for his Brother's anus and penis, and for the wrists which had been bound, and for Yeshua's mouth which had been tied. Issa gave to him laudanum, Poppy extract, while yet the Poppies from this season fluttered with their precious papery petals in the fields all about them, their medicine both rest and beauty.

III.18

And Yeshua rested and slept deeply, and was not healed.

I ssa knew that his greatest understanding as a Healer was in Silence, and so he journeyed beside his wounded Twin, still, and clear, listening, looking and seeking, for the holy, everywhere about them, in the wisdom of this Silence and mercy and love, shepherding his tender Twin on his journey to quest for the sacred in life, that Yeshua might follow that path for which he had been born.

Together they regarded the crescent Moon and the flight of egrets across the rose~lit sky. They felt the ripples of breeze upon the sand and the stream, the waving of grasses and wheat, and the warming and cooling of dawns and dusks. They heard the sounds of crickets and songbirds, of camels and young Children at play.

III.20

And then one day, as Issa sat, gently turning to regard the sights of a marketplace, and they partook a midday meal, Issa was in the Silence. And, as he turned back, he saw that his Brother had taken half of their food and was rising to carry it across the square to a young woman who had been placed outside of the village life by disease. And Issa learned from his Twin.

And he knew that his Twin, Yeshua, had been healed.

.

III.21

They crossed the Ganges at Varanasi, and quietly bore witness to the prayers of those dying, those seeking, those pregnant, newly wed, those with offerings of Marigolds, ghee, fruits and nuts, to the Gods, the ancestors, the mountains, the mystery. Yeshua was excited, so much color, such vibrancy, so many concepts of the Sacred, names of the Divine, the chants calling out in sonorous rhythmic tone, musicianship and instrumentation, strings, drums, cymbals, and voices.

And so Issa enjoyed, for the first time, a prayer that came from the Silence as did he, and he began his morning with the sound of the Gayatri Mantra in his soul and heart, his ear and voice, and he was content.

Aum

Bhur buvah svaha

Tat savitur vareniyam

Bhargho devasya dhimahi

Dhiyo yo nah prachodhayat

Aum

III.22

Yeshua explored Brahman, Vishnu, Siva, Saraswati, Durga, Lakshmi, Hanuman, and Ganesha, the Vedas, Rishis, and ceremonies. He meditated, offered, prayed, and sang, fasted and feasted, wore white and saffron. He realized that the One whom he had been taught to revere in Silence, Yhwh, was the One from whom all these many names and forms of joy and meaning came.

He realized all religions, all faiths, given language and form, were seeking, were speaking, the same quest for peace and truth, for meaning and expression, for beauty and for grace, manifest in our sacred lives, our precious lives, as humans, upon this one Earth, together.

Issa was told of a great Temple complex, in the province of Orissa, a week's walk. It was once part of the pantheistic history of Northeastern India, the Bengal peoples, then converted to a renowned Buddhist Temple, tended by monks of the original generation of Gautama Buddha's students, and then to Hinduism, the many~faced tradition of Deities and manners of prayer for all, tended by the Brahmin Priests anointed to pray for all who came to worship, to seek, to initiate the various rites of passage of the human life, from seeking conception, to birth, maturation, marriage, contemplation, health, prosperity, wisdom, and death.

They arrived amid the Ratha Yatra, a great procession of ancient statues in the baulm of the Bay of Bengal.

III.24

The Brothers walked through Calcutta, city at the river's mouth, and turned South to Puri. And there they beheld the complex where Yeshua was to study. Within, upon the central altar, stood two diminutive statues of dark stone: one a woman, one a man, side by side, equal, in the form of Marriage, the Marriage of all souls to the Creator, all souls equal yet different, set upon this Earth to seek a path of the holy in life, in all of life. The Temple itself was constructed in the form of the Vedic Wedding ceremony, the oldest written form of prayer upon the Earth. And Yeshua rested.

As Yeshua spent his days in prayer and contemplation, thought and profound feeling, sentiment and sensate practice, from perfumed oils and offerings, to music and Silent meditation, circumambulation and shawl-covered shoulders at the evening Arati service, his very days, his very life itself, were ceremonies to his Father in Heaven, and he was perceived as a good man, a holy man, this man with the face of an Angel, and the heart of a wounded Saint.

Issa observed many illnesses unknown to the people of his heritage, and he took care that the water and food of which his Brother partook was clean and blessed. One day he witnessed a Mother bring her Babe, seemingly lifeless in her strong young arms, and leave the Baby outside the door at the foot of the altar room of the Jagannath, the great Temple complex, at the side which would be the woman's side. The Baby had maggots in a wound on the left leg, feces in the cloth about the body. The Babe was unconscious, sick unto death it would seem. And everyone stayed away from the Baby and moved in their ablutions, prostrations and prayers away from the disease possible at this young Babe's birth and life and death. Such bad karma: some sins in Mother, Father, Babe, Ancestor, destiny.

And the Priests sent for someone to come and carry the young Babe to where he or she belonged, in a place unclean, for burial or garbage.

I ssa arose, Son of the Creator of Silence, Son of the Silence itself, Son of the One, quietly strode to the Baby, gathered the Babe into his great arms and carried the little one away from the complex into the open courtyard before it, behind the booths of garland makers and coconut vendors, mala artisans and carvers of statues, shawl sellers and tea shops.

For an hour, he tended the tiny Child, bathing, baulming, poulticing, and plucking, until the Child was clean, oiled, and free from parasites upon its skin, with medicines which Issa knew given from the little bag at his side and from Issa's fingertips into the mouth of the tiny one. He wrapped the Child in his own shawl as the day grew toward evening.

And the tiny one's eyes opened, and the Babe was healed.

The Mother had remained present at a distance, to know what this strange one was doing with her dying Baby, her dead Baby, her Baby whose spirit could no longer hold itself to life. The young Mother sought to know, as she left the Babe at the Goddess's side of the Temple, what the Priests and the janitors would do, to see with her loving eyes and be with her Mother's senses, how they might carry her beloved first~born away to the ghats, to the pit, to the garbage, upon a shovel or broom, or an old tarp, but please, blessed into Heaven's care at this holy place, away from the dogs, and not abandoned nor desecrated.

'Please, Goddess, please.'

When the Baby moved and was alive and would be well, and Issa finally gently smiled in his tender, grave face, the Mother fainted.

The Mother awoke to find Issa beside her, an old woman as well, a woman persuaded by Issa that the Mother and Baby were not ill with something which would harm her. And so, the old woman helped the Mother to arise, and Issa placed the Baby into the faithful, loving Mother's arms, and he quietly walked to Yeshua's and his home, the room which they rented during this time, in Puri, near the Anadaman Sea on the Bay of Bengal.

Several months later, as Issa walked by the Sea, he knew in the Silence that there was danger. He walked to the Temple and found that there was rumor which had begun, as Yeshua instructed all, wealthy landowner, and moderate vendor, warrior, and farmer, and now, woman, and those men and women whose work was that of the desecrations of life, unclean, that of sewage and death.

Yeshua had walked through a doorway forbidden still in this World. And the rumors were of his planned death, to be paid for by several Priests of the Buddha and of the Hindu and regional Deities and ways in coins of silver. The pure Priests tended their work in prayer and grace, as good men will do, but the several who could not bear Yeshua's ways turned away from holiness, at Jagannath, in Puri, the great Temple, of many layers of culture and of varied faiths over many centuries.

Yeshua turned to find his Twin beside him, at the Temple courtyard. Without words, Issa gestured to his Brother that he thirsted, for them to take something together. Yeshua's students stepped back, for everyone knew of the Healer, the quiet one.

So, Yeshua stopped his teaching to sit and share food and drink with his Brother, a splendid midday meal, a blessed meal, and Issa brought Yeshua back to their room, where they packed their few belongings and walked North and just to the West, to the area of Temples at the foot of the Himalaya.

III.32

The journey was filled with beauty, from the scents of the season in the plants and Trees, to places they had known and learned and wondered. They walked for some time in the area where Gautama Buddha had studied, and they prayed and contemplated his great soul, his penetrating heart and mind, his life of dedication to all, from men to women to deer to Trees, and rivers and sky.

And they came to the small city of precious Temples, Temples and Shrines of several faiths, with beautiful markets and homes, with gentle peoples, the Nepali, and the Sherpa, and visiting people from China, Tibet, the Stans, and the West. This was a crossroads between mountain and valley, plain, city and country, this place of peace and trade, holiness and humanity.

III.34

This was a place of cold at Winter's turn, so the Twins sought warm shawls and covering for their bodies and feet. They found a merchant of fine repute with yak boots and robes, and as the merchant's Daughter turned to measure Yeshua, Issa saw that this was love for his Twin, in the visages of his Brother and the brave and lovely young woman.

Such a noble Family. Such sacred fortune.

III.35

Through the days, Yeshua studied the many faces of God at the Temples, Shrines and Monasteries, the many ways in which humanity sought and named the sacred. He courted Sura in the late afternoons and began to be invited to take the evening meal with her Family. The months turned toward Winter and the time of the trails in the Himalaya bound by ice and snow, wherein trade quieted for the year. The Family looms were kept weaving, cloth embroidered with silk and woolen threads by the firelight.

III.36

And Issa addressed all who came to him, who were brought to him. He birthed, he tended wound and pneumonia, disease and distress, parasite and the broken cheekbone of a beaten Wife, advising her Husband to work away in the mountain huts with the yaks and goats where he was able and happy, and not in the city where this man of the mountain village could not cope without violence.

Issa tended a Child's dogbite, and infections, an aging man's pain in his chest as his heart beat toward the Heavens, and the abscess of teeth in the old man's Wife.

As a virulence passed through the village after a trader came through from an infected city, so many fell ill that Issa had to pace his own sleep and rest, his own cleansing of his mouth and body, his own food and drink, that he stay strong and clear, able to tend all who were brought to him, who found their way to him, to this man of Silence.

And in this plague the Sister of Sura fell gravely ill, so ill, that no one believed she might live.

And Issa did the unknowable.

He came into the house of Sura's Family, and placed his lambskin blanket upon the ground before the fire, and he slept, having placed the body of the Sister, the little one, at the fire several feet away from himself. And in the morning, her little face, and throat, and chest, and hands, and feet, sweated as if the very fever of the World were pouring forth from her. And Issa rose and tended her, cleansing her sweet face and body as if she were his own Child.

And the girl lived.

And Sura's Father knew he might allow Yeshua to marry his Sura, such a Family from which Yeshua came, this Brother of Issa. Surely his Sura would be safe, and well, so very far away, so very, very far away.

With such a Husband and such a Family.

There were three flowers in bloom as Spring turned to warm the Himalayan Southern slopes, and the snow and ice of the high peaks and glaciers began its clear, clean roar down from the heights to the valleys~avalanche, stream, waterfall. Forever after, Issa thought of those three flowers as the flowers of Sura, although he did not know their names in her language or in any language. They were embedded in the Silence of his great soul, these flowers of his young Sister~in~Law, the Wife of his tender, wounded Twin.

The Wedding was held at the Temple of her Family's prayer and tradition, with ceremony in their language, their beauty, their ways. The Bride was as beautiful as the flowers of her signature, and her Mother wept, as Mothers will do~her Daughter destined to travel so far, so very far away.

There would be a blessing and offerings given at the Temple upon return to Jerusalem, and together, the Twins prayed in the manner of their Family, humbly, truly, in great dignity and honor.

There was food and celebration. The day was holy and filled with the love of God in all of His names.

III.39

Three weeks after the Wedding day, Issa approached the Father of Sura with the promise that he would safely care for her to their Mother's home ~ their Mother, who would welcome the new Bride, his Daughter, as her own Daughter. Their Mother, still young, gentle, firm, so very good. There was to be no concern, no worry, no loss.

Parcels would be sent by caravan twice to several times annually. Issa knew, had learned, several Families who held routes traded over centuries among tribes across all borders, through all weathers, in great trust and goodness. The packages could be counted upon to be sent ~their Daughter's embroidery, items from Jerusalem, items from the Groom's village~and a message with all news regarding the couple and their marital Family. Thus, the Mother might know, seeing the familiar style of stitch and weave of fabric, the very nature and mood of their Daughter's wellbeing.

The Father was at peace.

Issa was certain for the three to be gone before a pregnancy could enter stages dangerous to the Bride. Issa, healing ever, from the Silence.

IV. RETURNING

IV.1

Items were packed, and the three turned from the Mother and Father, the Family, and treasured valley of people and Shrines, of traditions and crossroads, and they journeyed to the West, as the dawn poured over the Eastern slope of the Himalaya.

The three crossed through areas of high mountain pass and many tribal peoples, and Yeshua traded with a kind artisan for earrings which Sura would wear with tenderness and love all of their lives. They feasted on yak and butter tea, nuts, ginger, and dried fruits, pomegranates, and barley.

Issa made a camp with his Twin each night, of their small tent of camel skin, and Sura set two rugs for the bridal bed within, and Issa took his great skin and lay his great soul and Healer's body outside of the tent, under the Stars.

And there was great meaning for them all.

They remained a week at Leh, then two, and three, almost four, no five, for Yeshua to be with the great Abbott, of whose wisdom he had heard since his Father, Josef, spoke to him of the Abbott and three men coming from afar to the Star at Yeshua's birth. The illustrious Abbott was almost blind, and very still, deeply still, from so many years of seeking, sitting, walking, chanting, reading, scriptures and prayers, blessings and ceremonies, the work of a holy man among his people. The ancient Sage dressed in saffron and crimson, with soft felted boots, and Yeshua slept at peace for the first time since his rape, so many, many months ago.

The one great Saint was healing baulm to the wound of the young Groom. The four men who had traveled to the birth beneath the Star counted one who had wounded Yeshua, one Saint of the Cedars of Lebanon and Syria, one now residing in the Heavens and no longer upon this Earth, and one whose course of holiness Yeshua might now follow, a spiritual Father, a true Saint. This fourth, this spiritual Father, this true Saint, was the Abbott, who had been, beneath that Star, a most tender young apprentice.

And Yeshua asked the Abbott's counsel regarding his great wound. Yeshua asked his blessing, his instruction. And the Abbott was pledged, on Earth and in Heaven, to heal him. And Issa prepared for the journey to the home of their Mother, Mary.

Sura gathered flowers to dry in the Middle Eastern Sun, and tied packets of them in scarves, for teas, tisanes, dyes, and cooking. When they stopped at villages, cities, and oases, she asked of the Families, the traders, the vendors, the spice bazaars; and Issa and Yeshua tended her with wry smiles and great heart, as she kept from being homesick by adopting her Mother's wisdom in seeking the ways of women in caring for cloth, food, nurturing, perfuming, storytelling, medicine, wisdom, strength, courage and kindness.

They loved her, Brother and Husband; they loved her.

IV.4

One day, as Issa obtained items for his pharmacopeia, Sura sat quietly with an elder woman, the Mother of the man with whom Issa was meeting for wisdom and medicines. Yeshua was away with the sacred men of the town, observing, seeking their manner of prayer and practice, respecting the people, regarding the people with honor and diligence, faith and great hope in the human soul and path. They were Zoroastrian, and Yeshua was greatly moved by their purity and quest, their daily practice, their Family life. He stood atop the Ziggurat, and in quiet awe regarded the sky and turned his soul and heart, his mind and hands toward his Father in Heaven, as he so loved to do, all days, every day.

Sura pulled a corner of her soft bridal shawl, embroidered by her beloved Mother, over her tender head, and Issa turned to see a teardrop at the side of her cheek, and a wayward curl of her hair, as the elder woman and he exchanged knowing glances, and the elder woman took Sura's hand in her own. Issa stood, and, placing a Brother's protective arm about Sura's shoulder, called her to her feet, and walked with her back to their camp. He helped her to lie down, with a blanket and tea, and he walked in Silence.

'Yeshua, please come. Your Sura is with Child.'

The camel was splendid, young and strong, and Sura rode for seven weeks upon his back, rolling in rhythm with his gait, finally cresting over the Golan and down into the precious valley of Galilee. Olive Trees and shimmering water of the inland Sea greeted her, a Daughter of the Himalaya, to this land of milk and honey.

Yeshua came to the doorway of his Family's home and lifted Sura from the splendid camel's back, as the camel kindly knelt. The doorway opened, and his Mother, Mary, came forth with tears and smiles, wisdom and worry, to greet her new Daughter and her new Daughter's Husband, Yeshua, her Son.

And Issa stood in the Silence, and Mary knew that Issa had seen many things. She knew Issa had kept his promise to Heaven and to her, and brought her Yeshua home.

Part Three

I am come forth from that mystery.

~The Pistis Sophia
Translation by G.R.S. Mead, 1921

V. BRINGING FORTH

V.1

It began in the village, at the inland Sea, in the hills, the teaching of so many beautiful concepts of the Divine, from afar, from traditions of lands far away, and from the traditions of this place, of his own people, his own heritage, the teaching of Yeshua to the peoples of the World.

He was happy, fulfilled, and of all faith, hope, and love, that humanity might realize the One from which all came, into which all would return, of which all were One, in the many, in the One.

Yeshua taught through the parables of which Josef, his Father, had taught him, that he might know ethics, and the value of truth and of the human ways of life, and of virtue and of seeking that which is the great way, the way among the Heavens, here upon the Earth.

The Babe came, on a cool night of early Spring, and for nights before, Issa slept and stayed outside beneath a great Tree by the home, as Sura quietly labored with Mary, and the wise woman from Lebanon came to midwife her birth.

They named the Child for Anna, and the Child was sublime.

There were three Children, over the decade of their youthful Marriage and precious life, and all were raised in the home of the woman whose womb was filled with grace, their Father's Mother, Mary. She walked with them to the well and taught them to pull the pail of clear, cool water up from the ropes, and to carry it home with them in their strong, young arms, to trade at market, to wash clothing and to dye ~ linen, wool and cotton, to cook, sweep, sing and pray. They were a Family of great meaning, a timeless Family, a holy Family.

Yeshua and Sura slept in the room beneath the great Tree, and they were fulfilled in all ways.

The boy was born at daybreak, and the Parents, the Grandmother, the village, celebrated, a boy, a Son, to carry forth the Family name, the land, the work. He was named for Sura's Father's Father and for Josef, and a missive was sent by caravan, with cloth spun and dyed and woven by Mary, and embroidered by Sura, of the news, the good news.

Two years later came the third Child, a second girl, so tender and sweet, that Baby of them all. To her, Mary taught the stories of her Family and people and the sacred crafts of her hands.

Part Four

If you ask peace, do not regard anyone's faults.
Regard one's own faults.
Learn to make the World one's own.
No one is a stranger, my Child.
The whole World is your own.

~Sarada Devi

VI. THE DARKNESS

VI.1

And then came the turn, the wound unhealed.

Those who sought to be known by the fame of the young Teacher brought Yeshua sweetmeats and praise, and there was one among them, a married woman, Mary, of Magdala, very beautiful, who wanted him, and wore new soft cloth and her hair down, perfumed, unveiled, when he would teach, when he would help, people from all across the region. She would stay away from her home and village, overnight, beneath the Trees, as Yeshua taught the circle of young men, Andrew, Peter, Bartholomew and Judah, Matthew, Mark, Judas, James the elder and James the younger.

And one night after all had gone to sleep, Mary of Magdala sought his counsel, away from the others.

And in the Autumn, the rumor began that she was carrying Yeshua's Child. She could be stoned.

As golden Poppies budded in the land below Jerusalem, Yeshua desired to journey to the great city, the city of David, and teach the peoples of the World who visited the great Temple, the regional Synagogues, the places of worship of other peoples from Assyria, Egypt, Ethiopia, Lebanon, Persia, Phoenecia, Syria, and many other lands, and the bazaars, the artisans, the food stalls and shops. There were schools for apprenticing Priests, Gardens, sacred springs and wells of history, and peoples from all over the known World.

Yeshua treasured his study in prayer, remembrance, respect and practice, and he wished to enter a mature study, a mature presentation, worthy of his heart's most fervent quest. His heart was heavy at Sura's distance from his soul. He was ashamed.

And so, on a bright Spring day, he bade his Family a fortnight's farewell, and turned upon an ass given him by a prosperous seeker who tended his parables and his talks upon the hillsides and at the village wells. Yeshua turned toward the great city, the city of his Bris, of his naming, and of his anointing into manhood.

Among the women expressed a rage that the young Teacher had betrayed Sura, so far from the home of her birth, such a Wife and Mother, such a Daughter~in~Law, such a woman. And rage toward Mary of Magdala, the beauty, the woman of formidable wealth and position, with Husband and Children, a fine home, servants and possessions.

That such a thing should come to pass with their Teacher.

Two of the women, Martha~the Sister of Mary of Magdala, and the Essene woman who was the Wife of Judas, spoke with their Husbands and asked the men to call this to the law, of the Elders, of the Synagogues, of village, of region.

And so it came to pass that at the very day upon which Yeshua rode through the gates of the city, the word of his adultery was spoken to the high Priest of the Temple of Jerusalem by the Priest's Wife, who was so very sad.

VII. THE SACRIFICE

VII.1

My Father entered the Garden of Gesthemane, beautiful Olive Trees on the hillside across the tender valley from the gates of Saint David's City, city of so many cultures, city of my Father being blessed in all the stages of his life's initiations. He found Issa irritated and vast, contemplative and Silent, awake in the Garden, with a handful, eight, of the men, devoted, who favored him, asleep amidst the Trees and grasses, rocks and pathways. Yeshua smiled at his Twin and nodded for him to go to the home of Magdalene in the city, for food, to wash, and to change. The men were asleep, and Issa asked Yeshua to go with him to Sura, and that all would be well, 'as it should be.'

Yeshua refused.

And Issa walked through the Lion's Gate into the City, and to a different home than that which held my Mother, and I in her womb.

And Issa, so often Silent, always in the intricacy of Eternity yet ever a human, had asked, 'Will not one of you remain awake with me an hour?' And none of them had done so. They had not seen, heard, tasted, touched, nor known, what happened. To all.

In mystery, sometime after my Father's death, Issa walked to the Himalaya. He lived. His soul is the key which blessed, which blesses, us all as One.

This will ever be.

When the soldiers came, Roman soldiers of the province, Yeshua was ready.

And so the tale we tell, throughout Christendom, of the one who so loved his Brother that he would give up his life for him. And who knew? Mary, who followed her Yeshua up the pathway, and knelt beneath the unwilling Trees carpentered into a cross from which he hung, her second~born, the one whom she nursed, whose infant body had called her from her bleeding and fatigue to nurse him at her breast. Magdalene, who carried me in her own womb, my Father upon those sad branches breathing his last so that Issa might remain the breath of life for us all.

I remember. I was there, of him, within her.

VII.4

Yeshua was raped this second time, by several of the Roman guards, a tactic generally used in war to desecrate the Sons and Wives, the Daughters and slaves, of the conquered. He was beaten, scourged, and crowned with a branch of thorns.

And in the morning he was called before Pontius Pilate. Adultery was not against the law of Rome.

VII.5

Pilate called Yeshua before the crowd, certain that the humiliation he had borne: semen, blood, feces and urine on his robe, buttocks and legs, blood and shredded skin across his beloved shoulders and down his back, sweat, dirt and tear~streaks across his face and cheeks, would resolve the sins caused the Priests of Yeshua's faith, his Wife and Family, the noted Husband of the refined woman with whom he had lain, the villages, the coming Babe.

But it did not suffice.

The crowd wanted death to the adulterer.

No one but Issa knew of the wound that had been with my Father since birth, the wise man who had wanted to be them, to be Issa and Yeshua, to possess them, and who had raped Yeshua and left him innocent yet broken into a shard of God's grace, a sacrifice for all men.

And that Mary of Magdala had somehow pulled upon that place in Yeshua to call him to her, so that he was taken by her will as well, my Father, Yeshua.

In Mary of Magdala's womb, in Jerusalem, that night, I waited to be born.

And so the next day came to pass, the day upon which the Roman Governor ordained my Father to walk, to carry a great cross of wood, up through the streets of Jerusalem, to a high place, to a place of death, to be nailed to the wood of that cross.

Yeshua was not allowed to be cleaned, but was ordered to remain covered in excrement and sperm, blood, scabs and flies, for all to see. He was not fed nor given water nor drink of any kind.

My Grandmother, Mary, the Mother of Yeshua, stood in her blue cloth~cloth woven at her loom~at her younger Twin's feet, throughout. And John, the elder wise Sage of our area, who honored my Father, studied with him, and studied with many holy men, as he had with the Baptist, my Father's cousin, before

John the Baptist was killed through another woman's treachery, stood, throughout.

And Mary of Magdala, brazen, in new red and ochre cloth, her russet hair down, perfumed and uncovered, with beautiful earrings, came to Yeshua's nailed feet, and Yeshua turned his head away from her toward his Mother. Mary of Magdala grasped at his feet, and beseeched him, and fell to her knees and wept, but he kept his face turned to his Mother, who forgave her Yeshua.

And a Roman soldier led Mary of Magdala away to the side. And the wise John embraced Mary, the Mother of my Father.

And Longinus, a Roman soldier known for his prowess, directed his lance into the side of my Father between his ribs and into his heart, so that he died, my Father, in peace.

My soul carried him to our Father in Heaven, and I lay in the womb of Mary of Magdala, so near my Father's tender body, so near my Grandmother, and waited to be born.

VII.7

Seven weeks later I was born in the wealthy home of Magdalene's Husband. My paternal Grandmother Mary paid a servant to take me at birth to the home of a Roman soldier whose Wife was my Grandmother's customer for woven cloth. The Family could not bear Children, and so I became their precious Daughter.

I never met my Grandmother nor did I see my Mother again.

My Roman Father was assigned to Glanum, in Occitania, in the Roman Provinces, of Gaul.

Part Five

And so, there was no need for the Crucifixion. I was awake with my Father for that hour, in my Mother's womb, and so we are here together.

VIII. RESURRECTION

VIII.1

Issa came to the grave and asked the soldiers for the body of his Twin. They rolled away the stone, and Issa carried his Brother from the grave to a safe place, where Yeshua was buried with prayer and anointing.

And in the morning, when Mary of Magdala came with ointment and herbs~although she had been asked to stay away~Issa, the Twin, stepped into the path and spoke to her.

'Yeshua!'

'Do not approach me. Do not touch me.'

And she found that the stone had been rolled away from the grave, and neither the soldiers nor the body were there.

Mary of Magdala ran to tell the others, 'I have seen him, He is risen.'

And so the cosmology began of Yeshua, my Father, as a God of the Sun, or a Son of God.

Issa quietly had marked his own hands and chest, his forehead, and trimmed his hair and beard in the style of his late Twin. He walked through Galilee and the surrounding areas for some ninety days, and taught in a different tone than that of his Brother, in his own tone, to heal and balance that which had been desecrated in their name, in the name of Sura, and Mary, and Josef, and Anna, and all, because of the heartbreaking wound within his Brother which had never been healed as it needed to be, from the man who had sought their power, their authority, their quiet path upon the Earth before men, the man who tried from their very birth to steal a destiny of all beings, the destiny of the Twins of the Star of Bethlehem.

But no one could have that destiny, that perfection of soul and heart as one yet two in my Father and my Uncle, which was and is and ever shall be, always.

IX. SANGREAL

IX.1

I ssa took five pouches from the work of his healing these many years.

One he sent with Martha to Occitania, and she stayed North at Tarascon, along the river above Avignon, and became known and revered for her wisdom and holiness. Her remains are buried there, in the depths of the Church.

The second he sent with Mary, his Mother, and an attendant to her, a farming widow in her last years. They journeyed to Samos, where the Greeks refused them, and then to Ephesus, where the Mother of a God was welcomed, even a defiled and sacrificed God.

His Mother passed her years high in the Trees among the hills above the port, a town dedicated to the Goddess Artemis, of whom it was rumored that Mary was an embodiment. People brought her food, and goods, oil lamps and candles, prayers and requests, and drank from the pure spring beneath her cottage. She wove, and prayed, and was holy and true before God and humanity.

The third and fourth he gave to Mary Jacobe and Mary Salome, and he hired the Boat of Bethany to sail the two apostolic Mothers of his Family and Sura safely to Occitania. There the three oppressed women landed and remained at the shore of the Sea, West of the river, in a village which became named for them, *Des Saintes Maries de la Mer.*

The Husband of Mary of Magdala sent her away after my birth, divorcing her in the Jewish law, in shame and ridicule, and she journeyed to Rome, where she attempted one last reach toward being the eternal consort of my Father. She spoke to the Roman Senate, in a flaming red robe with her burnished hair down, glorious in her beauty, her jewelry and perfume; and she was admired and thought possibly a Goddess, formidable in courage, intelligence and manner. She journeyed West to Occitania, where the women of her life in Palestine would not receive her. So, she is rumored to have entered a cave at the massif above Saint Maximum de la Baume, a village settled among its traditional people by Maximum, a student of my Father sympathetic to my Mother's destiny and history. Mary of Magdala's last years were spent within the village, in the gentle, strong care of Maximum, in Provincia Romana.

And the giving of the fifth pouch broke the heart of Issa.

He gave the pouch unto the Children of his Twin, and sent them by Sea to join their Mother Sura, who had gone ahead to prepare a way for them, and to make certain the paths of such foreign people would be held safe and true in such a land and among the Gauls, Romans and others of the Province. The three Children of Yeshua and Sura came into the Camargue and lived there until grown, with their Mother and the two Saints Maries, these three Children, the legitimate Daughters and Son of Yeshua.

The elder Daughter married young and was killed, very heavy with Child, with a great long knife, while she was gathering Autumn herbs in the beautiful, beautiful coastal plain of the Camargue. She was killed brutally, brutally by one of the men who feared rumors that one of the Children of the young Teacher might bear a Messiah~a Second Coming spoken of by Yeshua, who had discoursed his curiosity of reincarnation and that he would come again, that he must, to fulfill the law. This elder Daughter had been pregnant with Twins, as is a path within the Family of my Grandmother Mary, also the Grandmother of this tragic, murdered, innocent young woman.

The young Mother's body, and those of her desecrated Babes, were anointed, and, as they aged, buried into a small sarcophagus, and over the path of many years' time, placed into the walls of a Church beneath a wooden statue of the Boat of

Bethany. From that time, seeking pilgrims touch the wall at the hidden bulge of the remains of the elder Daughter and her Twins.

Her Mother, Sura, many years later, was buried, and this Church was built above Sura's remains. The Church was composed in the very shape of the Boat of Bethany. The altar to God and Heaven was built above her sarcophagus, the grave of the Daughter of the Himalaya and Galilee and France.

IX.4

The younger Daughter never healed. Never wed.

The Son was shepherded in the year after the murder, quietly, without missive nor message to anyone, to the North of Gaul and across the straits to the West, to Glastonbury in Britannia Major, among the sacred peoples who were cousins to the Essenes, who loved the study of mystery, who admired the sacred in so many forms of the men and women of the World. And from there the Son was shepherded to Corca Dhuibhne in the Southwest of Hibernia, to the Northwest tip of the precious peninsula, where he was wed to the Daughter of a Druid Priest. There they dwelled, raised their loving Family, tended the land and animals; and he was trained by his Father~in~Law, in holiness, goodness, joy and humble human meaning.

I was wed at age twelve to a Roman aristocrat, who was fascinated by my abundant auburn hair, features, nubile body and charm, my education and my place as an only Child in a kind Family of military meaning and repute. I became pregnant with my late Father at age thirteen, just as had my Grandmother, Mary, and I bore him quietly and named him in my heart, although my Husband named him a noble Roman name before the Gods and man. We dwelled in great harmony for many years and were blessed with three other Children, until a serving maid seduced my Husband and turned him to unconscious displeasure toward his kin and care.

My Son fell ill of a damp cold, having been poisoned, and this turned to an unwillingness to be alive through betrayal, so he left us, and I followed him soon after.

Our souls remained with the great remembrance that the Second Coming could have been at Glanum, at the foot of the Luberon, so precious, amid Lavender and Poppy, Grapevine and Pine.

And in the Silence, Issa, still in his mood, steady in his footstep, unafraid, serene, internally poised, turned to the Himalaya, until he, his Twin, and I, would return to embody the coming prophesied throughout all time and space, forth from, into, and of, the Great Mystery.

Postscript

1. The Gayatri Mantra is founded upon a verse from the Rg Veda, our oldest written word upon the Earth:

Aum
Bhur buvah svaha
Tat savitur vareniyam
Bhargho devasya dhimahi
Dhiyo yo nah prachodhayat
Aum

>   ~Brahmarshi Vishvamitra

Translation:

Om

The terrestrial, celestial, and that between, are offered

That All Creating One, Most Venerated

We meditate upon the Self~luminous radiance of the Divine

Inspiring our actions, properties and intellect

Om

2. Men and women have conducted formal and informal scholarship across two millennia including:

In the Early Centuries after the lives of the Holy Family:

>   *The Apocrypha*
>   *The Books of Jeu*
>   *The Dead Sea Scrolls*
>   *The Gnostic Gospels, including the Nag Hammadi Library*
>   *The Infancy Gospel of Thomas*
>   *The Pistis Sophia*
>   *The Valentinian Gnostic Gospel*

In the early Nineteenth Century:

> *Research expedition of the Ramakrishna lineage of Bengal, India, to the Monastery of Leh, as assigned by Sarada Devi*
>
> *Research of Russian philosopher and artist Nicholas Roerich*

In the Twentieth Century:

> *The Works of G.R.S. Mead*
>
> *The Cathar Texts, including The Cathar Ritual (Lyon Ritual) The Book of the Two Principles, Interrogatio Iohannis (Questions of John)*

3. The Grail is revered as that mystical blessing which is within the empty cup of grace utilized in prayer, ceremony, and supping at the renowned Last Supper, although some have focused upon the literal physical cup.

And the Grail is revered as that living grace present within the descendants of the Children of Yeshua, now within millions of people's DNA throughout our world, thus held in blessing and life among our human holy Family.

4. From the Pistis Sophia, also from the Berlin Codex and the Nag Hammadi:

> *Again, his disciples said, 'Tell us clearly how they came down from the invisibilities, from the immortal to the world that dies.' The perfect Savior said, 'Son of Man consented with Sophia, his consort, and revealed a great androgynous light. Its male name is designated Savior, begetter of all things. Its female name is designated All~Begettress Sophia. Some call her 'Pistis.''*

> ~Ascribed to Yeshua as the transfigured Christ

5. The Hopi Native North American Tribe embodies tradition ascribing to the Earth two saviours, elder and younger Twin souls, 'Brothers.' The two hold a key shepherding Earth and humanity, have incarnated before, and, in every era, as a Messiah. Tradition represents that if people come with a cross as their spiritual signature, they are to be welcomed with kindness, but not to be believed, because they do not know who they are. If people come with a cross within a circle, the younger and elder Twins, they are to be welcomed as Family.

A cross within a circle is held by many Native Tribes of the Americas as a Medicine Wheel of all life and of all people.

ABOUT THE AUTHOR

On the 25th day of November, 1953, Elizabeth Anne Hin
was born in Corning, New York, unto her parents,
Teresa Helen Wenderlich and William Arie George Hin,
by Dr. James J. Mulcahy.